EVERY SECRET THING

Judy GeBauer

BROADWAY PLAY PUBLISHING INC
New York
www.broadwayplaypublishing.com
info@broadwayplaypublishing.com

EVERY SECRET THING
© Copyright 2011 by Judy GeBauer

Cover image by Suzanne Coley
First printing: December 2011
I S B N: 978-0-88145-507-6
Book design: Marie Donovan
Page make-up: Adobe Indesign
Typeface: Palatino
Printed and bound in the U S A

EVERY SECRET THING was developed by Chameleon Stage, Denver. It then premiered in June 2007 at Modern Muse Theater Company (Stephen J Lavezza, Executive Artistic director; Gabriella Cavallero, Artisitic Director) in Denver. The cast and creative contributors were:

RICHARD PACKARD ....Gregory J Adams
BARBARA PENNING.............................. Gabriella Cavallero
ANDY LAWTON.. Josh Hartwell
DREW BAXTER.. Jim Hunt
MAXINE HOYT ....Jessica Posner
AGENT KIMBLE.. Jono Waldman

Director, set & sound design .... Stephen J Lavezza
Costume design....................................Mallory Kay Nelson
Lighting design ....Rob Byers
Stage manager...Gregory L Melton

CHARACTERS & SETTING

RICHARD PACKARD, *30, a junior high Civics teacher*
BARBARA PENNING, *late 20s, a junior high Music teacher*
ANDY LAWTON, *late 20s, a junior high English teacher*
DREW BAXTER, *40s, a junior high school principal*
MAXINE HOYT, *14, a junior high school student*
AGENT KIMBLE, *30s, F B I*

Time: 1954

Place: Classrooms and faculty lounge
BAXTER's *office*
KIMBLE's *office*

Note: The play's multiple locales should be suggested and represented as minimally as possible.

The passage of days and weeks is denoted by teachers writing the new date on the chalk board

Excerpt from Dulce et Decorum Est *public domain*
Excerpt from Shenandoah *public domain*
Excerpt from Last Lines *public domain*

ACKNOWLEDGMENTS

Thank you Gene and Amber
for everything
and
thanks to Modern Muse for your
dedication to new work

For God shall bring every work into judgment with every secret thing whether it be good or evil
Ecclesiastes 13:14

ACT ONE

(Light on RICHARD *holding a document)*

RICHARD: *(Reads)* "I do solemnly swear or affirm that I will support the Constitution of the United States ...

(Light on MAXINE *holding a document)*

MAXINE: *(Reads)* Amendment One.

RICHARD: *(Reads)* ...that I am not a member of the Communist Party or under any oath...

MAXINE: *(Reads)* Congress shall make no law respecting an establishment of religion or abridging the freedom of speech...

RICHARD: *(Reads)* ...or a party to any agreement or under any commitment that is in conflict with my obligations under this oath.

MAXINE: *(Reads)* ...or of the press, or the right of the people to peaceably assemble...

(Light out on MAXINE*)*

RICHARD: *(Reads)* I further swear or affirm that I do not advise, advocate, or teach..."

(He hesitates, then signs it)

(Faculty room. RICHARD *at table with stack of report folders.* BARBARA *is at table also, with coffee and musical score. She hums from Prokoviev's* Kije*)*

BARBARA: Did you tell Sandy about Hawaii?

RICHARD: Hmmm-mmm.

BARBARA: She excited?

RICHARD: You know.

BARBARA: Just wait till she gets there.

RICHARD: She's glad we're going. It's hard for her right now.

BARBARA: You can try again. The doctor didn't say she couldn't have another …

RICHARD: We're not quite ready.

BARBARA: Have you been to the Islands before?

RICHARD: First time for both of us.

(BARBARA *and* RICHARD *return to their work.*)

(*Silence*)

BARBARA: Richard…

RICHARD: Hmmm…

BARBARA: Did you…sign the…loyalty…? I shouldn't ask.

RICHARD: Yeah, I signed. You?

BARBARA: I couldn't think of a good reason to refuse.

RICHARD: I could think of a few practical reasons not to.

BARBARA: I think Andy's considering refusing.

RICHARD: So he says.

BARBARA: You think he's grandstanding?

RICHARD: No, but you know Andy.

(*Enter* ANDY *carrying his brief case and a movie magazine.*)

ANDY: Look what I confiscated in home room. A question for the ages. "Why Marilyn Will Not Marry Marlon Brando." (*He tosses magazine on table.*)

RICHARD: Boy, I was wondering.

BARBARA: Maybe because she's married to Joe DiMaggio.

RICHARD: Maybe Marlon didn't ask her.

ANDY: And alliterative, too.

BARBARA: "Will Kirk Douglas Leave Home?" My God, what next.

ANDY: Oh, how about "Susan's Studio Stand-off."

RICHARD: And alliterative, too.

ANDY: *(Reads)* "Susan Hayward is no stranger to trouble. Her mercurial career in Tinseltown has been plagued with fights with studio bosses and agents. But her current battle with Twentieth Century-Fox may leave this talented actress out in the cold. Meanwhile, her up-and-down marriage to Jess Barker..." Oh well. She'll work it out. Susan's tough. *(He sits and snaps open case on his lap and takes out copy of school newspaper.)* Anybody pick up this week's *Fandango* yet?

BARBARA: Not yet.

ANDY: Well, the noon movie this week is *El Paso*.

BARBARA: Could it be a western?

ANDY: Sterling Hayden is the villain menacing John Payne and Gail Russell. Mary Beth Hughes plays Stage Coach Nellie. Oh boy. I better catch this one. I'm a big Mary Beth fan.

BARBARA: Did they announce the auditions for my music assembly in there?

ANDY: Yep, right here. Right alongside the Sadie Hawkins dance. The term play will be *Madwoman of Chaillot*.

RICHARD: You know, every now and then these kids amaze me.

ANDY: I'll say. Giraudoux is pretty hip stuff for junior high actors.

RICHARD: No, I mean here. This assignment I gave my civics class. A research paper on a government agency of their choice. This girl wanted F B I but it was taken, so she took Secret Service and she comes up with this snappy Q and A, as though she's actually meeting an agent for lunch and interviewing the guy about his job. *(He reads from paper:)* "I didn't know what sort of person to expect and was very surprised when the man who sat down at my booth was dressed in a suit and loafers just like my dad wears to work.
"We don't try to look like Secret Service agents," he told me.
"Because you're spies," I said.
"No. In another country the secret service might be spies. We're an agency of the Treasury Department. We go after counterfeiters and we protect the President."
"What if you got a tip that somebody wants to kill the President? Would you bug their phone line? One good way I know about to catch criminals is to write down license numbers of their friends so you can keep tabs on them."

ANDY: Slightly unconstitutional.

BARBARA: How would a kid know to do that?

ANDY: Television is amazing.

RICHARD: *(Continues reading)*
"How do you catch someone who wants to kill the President?"
"Room 98."
He didn't say anymore, so I had to ask him what that was."

Anyway, her whole paper's like that. Really imaginative.

BARBARA: Well?

RICHARD: Well?

ANDY: What's Room 98?

RICHARD: It's where they sift through death threat letters to the President. She does a wonderful job here of describing the whole process. And you should hear her on counterfeiting. Funny money, she calls it.

BARBARA: Who is this student?

RICHARD: Maxine Hoyt.

ANDY: Oh yes. Maxine. Of course. Who else?

RICHARD: She's a great student. You have problems with her?

BARBARA: She's not a problem student at all. More the opposite.

ANDY: Bit of an eager-beaver.

BARBARA: I have her in music. She sings in Glee. She has a nice voice, she's a pleasant kid, she does the work. I just notice that she's unusually intense. Gung-ho. Is that the word?

ANDY: Evangelical. She's an academic ecstatic. Last week, Friday of last week, each kid in my Eighth Grade English had to choose a poem and prepare it and present it in front of the class.

(Light on MAXINE*)*

MAXINE: *(Recites poem with relish)*
If in some smothering dreams, you too could pace
Behind the wagon that we flung him in,
And watch the white eyes writhing in his face,
If you could hear, at every jolt, the blood
Come gurgling from the froth-corrupted lungs,

Bitten as the cud
Of vile, incurable sores on innocent tongues,
My friend, you would not tell with such high zest
To children ardent of some desperate glory,
The old lie: *Dulce et decorum est*
Pro patria mori.

(Light on ANDY. *This is his English class.)*

ANDY: Do you know what the Latin means?

MAXINE: "It is sweet and fitting to die for your country." I take Latin.

ANDY: Owens speaks about "children ardent of some desperate glory". What is ardor? What does he mean?

MAXINE: Ardor?

ANDY: Did you look up the word?

MAXINE: I can look it up right now. I meant to look it up. I really meant to.

ANDY: You seem rather "ardent" about the gruesome aspects of this poem.

MAXINE: I do?

(Light out on MAXINE.*)*

ANDY: It was good work. Good choice of poem. But her panic when she didn't know the answer. And there was something about the way she read it. It was the … the relish…the zeal…the…

BARBARA: The ardor.

(Enter BAXTER, *very distressed.)*

BAXTER: I'm calling an emergency faculty meeting this afternoon. I'm very sorry. You'll all have to stick around. Awfully short notice. Can't be helped.

RICHARD: What's up?

BAXTER: Sven Larsen.

Silence)

ANDY: Yeah?

BARBARA: Has something happened to him?

BAXTER: He's been called before the… He's supposed to appear…

(Silence)

RICHARD: Jesus.

BAXTER: It's not necessarily bad news.

ANDY: Being subpoenaed before the House committee isn't bad news?

BAXTER: It's not the House committee.

RICHARD: The Senate?

BAXTER: Let's keep good thoughts. It's only…uh…

BARBARA: Only what?

ANDY: Drew!

BAXTER: It's a kind of sit-down.

RICHARD: Sit-down?

BAXTER: On a local level.

RICHARD: With…?

BAXTER: Now let's not… The F B I.

BARBARA: He's a math teacher.

RICHARD: What could the F B I possibly want with Sven Larsen?

BAXTER: I'll tell you what I can at the faculty meeting. I feel we should form a united front, support Sven in every way we can.

ANDY: A coffee klatch. With the F B I.

RICHARD: When is he called?

BAXTER: He's there right now. This whole thing is terribly … Emergency meeting right after dismissal. Pass it on. And Andy, I still need you to sign the… *(He starts to leave and sees the movie magazine.)* "Elizabeth Taylor's Moment of Truth."

ANDY: Yeah, they asked her to sign the loyalty oath.

(BAXTER exits.)

(Silence)

RICHARD: Sven Larsen.

ANDY: My God, that poor guy.

(BARBARA, very distressed, grabs the magazine, opens and reads.)

BARBARA: "Deborah Kerr, with husband Anthony Bartley, who was one of the courageous Few during World War Two, was in town for Blah blah blah… Her two daughters came to the studio with her and enjoyed watching Mom try on Edith Head's creations…" *(She slams the magazine down.)*

ANDY: It's got to be some kind of mistake.

RICHARD: Okay, now just let's not get… He has his citizenship.

ANDY: So does Dalton Trumbo. So does Dashiell Hammett.

BARBARA: You think it has something to do with his European background?

ANDY: He probably studied at the "wrong" university. Had the "wrong" math professor.

RICHARD: They'll clear it up.

BARBARA: Algebra. Geometry. How subversive is a protractor?

ANDY: You have any idea how many Sven Larsens there must be?

BARBARA: How could he even come to their attention in the first place?

RICHARD: They probably check everyone who became a citizen after the war. This has got to be routine.

BARBARA: He's got a boy going here, doesn't he.

RICHARD: That's right. Alex.

(Silence)

ANDY: Nosebleed.

BARBARA: What?

ANDY: Nosebleed! Nosebleed!

RICHARD: Oh… Uh… Excuse me. Excuse… (He hurries from the room.)

BARBARA: Here's some Kleenex.

ANDY: Thanks.

BARBARA: Tip your head back. Okay? Better?

ANDY: What are they doing to poor old Sven?

BARBARA: Keep your head tilted.

ANDY: Right now he's sitting in some office being…

BARBARA: He doesn't have a mark against him. He'll be fine.

ANDY: His poor family.

BARBARA: He'll be just fine. You need more?

ANDY: It's stopping. Thanks.

BARBARA: I don't think I've had a bloody nose in years.

ANDY: You're not Polish.

BARBARA: I didn't know you were Polish. Lawton?

ANDY: Oh, you know. Immigration got it wrong.

BARBARA: Look, Andy, I hate to leave you like this, but I've got to get this work done before that darned meeting this afternoon. I'm going back to my classroom. I'll see you later. You be okay? *(Pause)* Andy, are you going to sign the oath?

ANDY: I sure hope Sven signed.

(RICHARD returns, begins to collect his stack of reports.)

RICHARD: Sorry. Emergency.

(Music by Mussorgsky plays.)

BARBARA: See you guys at the faculty meeting. "Pass it on."

(Music continues.)

(Lights on classroom areas. It is the following day. Teachers write the new date on their chalk boards.)

ANDY: *(Reads)* No coward soul is mine
No trembler in the world's storm-troubled sphere
I see Heaven's glories shine
And faith shines equal, arming me from fear.

(He writes on chalk board: "Last Lines" and "Emily Brontë")

RICHARD: *(Lectures)* If you think of court as a stage and the trial as a kind of play, then each of the characters has a specific function in the play.

BARBARA: *(Lectures)* Mussorgsky is a turbulent and rather tragic figure. Born in Karevo in 1839. Died in Saint Petersburg, now called Leningrad, in 1881. Many of his works were never finished because of his nervous disposition and dependence on alcohol. A very sad man.

ANDY: These were the last lines Emily Brontë ever wrote. Emily Dickinson thought so much of her poetry that she chose this poem to be read at her own funeral.

(RICHARD writes on the board as he lectures.)

RICHARD: We have the judge. We have the prosecuting and defense attorneys. We have witnesses. We have the court clerk. The bailiff. We have a plaintiff. And last but not least, the defendant.

BARBARA: But those of his works that survive are among our most cherished classical treasures.

ANDY: Emily Brontë lived and wrote in what we call the Victorian period. Most people think of that time as prudish and repressed and old fashioned. But actually it was a very complex age.

RICHARD: As we begin our study of the judicial system, you will see why we spent so much time on the Bill of Rights at the beginning of the semester.

BARBARA: "Pictures at an Exhibition" and "Night on Bald Mountain" are the two Mussorgsky compositions most western audiences will recognize. Just listen.

ANDY: Think about this. What Victorian literary form parallels Elizabethan drama in terms of popularity and literary achievement?

(*Music continues.*)

RICHARD: Let's consider the Fifth Amendment. Remember from our discussions, the Fifth provides that a defendant does not have to give testimony that will incriminate him. The Fifth also states that a defendant found not guilty may not be tried again for the same crime, even if evidence is later uncovered that proves his guilt.

MAXINE: That's double jeopardy!

RICHARD: Thank you, Maxine. Don't forget to raise your hand.

(BAXTER *enters* RICHARD'*s classroom.*)

BAXTER: Mister Packard? See you outside?

RICHARD: Class, please review the First and Fifth Amendments. I'll be right outside the door. *(He steps aside with* BAXTER.*)* Listen, Drew, I'd like to discuss the loyalty oath pros and cons in class.

BAXTER: My office. After the bell.

RICHARD: It's really relevant to—

BAXTER: Dick, do not rock any boats right now. Immediately after the bell. Sorry I interrupted.

(Exit BAXTER. RICHARD *turns back to his class.)*

RICHARD: Okay. Fifth Amendment. Much in the news lately. How does the Fifth apply to the judicial set-up we have here? Our system presumes innocence. Very important that you understand this. The defendant does not have to prove innocence. The prosecutor has to prove guilt.

ANDY: Victorians had a strong sense of social responsibility which differed from their predecessors, the Romantics. Matthew Arnold criticized a bishop who discovered and published mathematical inconsistencies in the Bible. Not because the bishop was wrong, but because Arnold felt that pointing this out to the general public was irresponsible.

(Light on BAXTER *in his office)*

BARBARA: You can hear in this music the composer's effort to come close to reality, to the upheaval of real life. The upheaval he may have been facing personally.

(Music out)

BAXTER: Dick, take a seat.

RICHARD: And since all defendants are presumed innocent, the Fifth is a most vital guarantor of our rights.

(RICHARD *turns into* BAXTER's *office area.)*

BAXTER: This won't take much time.

RICHARD: I think I'd rather stand.

BAXTER: This is no big deal.

RICHARD: You sounded pretty urgent.

BAXTER: Really. Please.

RICHARD: You called me out of class.

BAXTER: Trust me.

RICHARD: I never trust anybody who tells me to trust them. Drew, now, you're not making eye contact.

BAXTER: Will you stop standing by the door?

RICHARD: Will you come to your point?

BAXTER: You were decorated for valor. *(Silence)* Distinguished Service Cross. *(Silence)* Did I say a bad word?

RICHARD: Drew, the war's over.

BAXTER: Is it true? *(Silence)* Is it true?

RICHARD: And if it is?

BAXTER: Will you please do me the courtesy of sitting down?

(RICHARD sits.)

BAXTER: You didn't mention it on any of your applications.

RICHARD: I didn't think it was relevant.

BAXTER: The Distinguished Service Cross isn't relevant? Audie Murphy has a Distinguished Service Cross.

RICHARD: I bet he doesn't put it on his résumé.

BAXTER: What I'm saying is a few good men have been given this award, and you are in their company—

RICHARD: I choose not to include it on my résumé. Was that all?

BAXTER: May one know why?

RICHARD: One may if one explained why one wants to know.

BAXTER: I've had a phone call.

RICHARD: Who from? Audie Murphy?

BAXTER: The Federal Bureau of Investigation.

RICHARD: Is it something about Sven Larsen?

BAXTER: They mentioned your decoration.

RICHARD: What do you mean, they mentioned it?

BAXTER: I wasn't even aware you'd been decorated.

RICHARD: Have they finished interviewing Sven? What did they want with him?

BAXTER: They're interested in uh, talking to you. So far as I know this has nothing to do with Sven.

RICHARD: Talking to me about what? *(He stands and paces.)*

BAXTER: They seem very impressed with your war record, which is apparently quite…impressive.

RICHARD: What do they want to see me about?

BAXTER: I didn't know you were in Italy.

RICHARD: It's not something I like to dwell on. Most guys don't. What do they want with me?

BAXTER: A chat.

RICHARD: A chat.

BAXTER: Naturally you're worrying about Sven's situation, but in your case…Dick, could you not prowl? It makes me awfully nervous.

RICHARD: A chat?

BAXTER: That's how they phrased it.

RICHARD: Why did they tell you and not me?

BAXTER: You'll receive a missive.

RICHARD: A missive.

BAXTER: Don't say it like that.

RICHARD: How did they say it?

BAXTER: The agent said missive.

RICHARD: Why don't I get a phone call? Why do I get a missive?

BAXTER: That was the word he used.

RICHARD: But he meant subpoena.

BAXTER: I don't think he meant that.

RICHARD: Oh yes you do.

BAXTER: I didn't get that impression.

RICHARD: Regardless of your impression, when the F B I gets in touch with you, it's a summons.

BAXTER: Hardly a summons.

RICHARD: Then why did you call me out of class?

BAXTER: Just an invitation.

RICHARD: So I can just R S V P. "Graciously declines. Previous commitments."

BAXTER: It should come anytime. He wanted me to know. As your superior.

RICHARD: I don't like the round-about, Drew. Okay, he contacted you, fine. You're the principal of the school where I teach. You should know they're calling me in. But I don't like that you knew before me.

BAXTER: I don't like it either.

RICHARD: Did you know before Sven Larsen? Did he get a missive?

BAXTER: This whole thing.

RICHARD: Not your fault, Drew. So, that it?

BAXTER: Let me know when you're scheduled to…

RICHARD: Assuming I accept their "invitation".

BAXTER: I'd cooperate. If I were you.

(RICHARD *starts to leave.*)

BAXTER: Why civics?

RICHARD: Civics?

BAXTER: You majored in philosophy, didn't you?

RICHARD: I'm sure you're aware of the abundant employment opportunities for philosophers.

BAXTER: So you changed your major to history? Sociology?

RICHARD: I'm not that interesting, Drew.

BAXTER: I am interested to know why you chose to teach civics.

RICHARD: Well, if you'd been in Italy …

(*Lights out on* RICHARD *and* BAXTER *and up on* MAXINE *in civics class*)

MAXINE: (*Reports with her usual zeal*) One of the most interesting cases the Secret Service worked on was when President Truman was nearly assassinated. This was only four years ago. See, the President wasn't living at the White House because it was being redecorated. So he lived across the street at a place called Blair House. It's a really nice old place but it's hard to protect the President there. It's right by the sidewalk and it doesn't have a fence or anything. So there was this agent patrolling the sidewalk and he heard a click like a gun and he turned around and there was this little guy pointing this pistol at him and he shot again and hit the agent in the leg. And then two other agents started firing and the assassin ran up the steps of the house and fired back at them and then one of the agents shot him in the chest. And the President was taking his nap and he heard gunfire so he ran to the window and the agents kept yelling to him to get back, get back. And then out of nowhere there's this other assassin.

(Light out on MAXINE*)*

*(*RICHARD *comes into the faculty room area where* ANDY *is reading a newspaper.)*

ANDY: Was that about Sven?

RICHARD: Was what about Sven?

ANDY: You're private with Drew.

RICHARD: Have you talked to Sven? How is he? How did it go?

ANDY: They practically accused him of being a personal friend of the Rosenbergs.

RICHARD: What'd they ask him?

ANDY: They grilled him.

RICHARD: Grilled him?

ANDY: He's really shaken up. They can't revoke his citizenship, can they?

RICHARD: He pays his taxes. He votes. He serves jury duty. He holds a steady job. What did they ask him? What kind of questions?

ANDY: That's right. He's a solid citizen. They can't deport him. Or…anything.

RICHARD: But they're through with him? He's in the clear?

ANDY: They think he may know someone.

RICHARD: What's that mean? Who does he know?

ANDY: They say he may know people who are … marginal, let's say. Under scrutiny. Sven's a cog in

a machine and probably an innocent cog but he ...
knows the wrong people.

RICHARD: They say he does? Or...he does?

ANDY: They want names. He can't...or won't...or...

RICHARD: Jesus. Do they have evidence? Witnesses?
Who is he supposed to know? He never attended any
meetings of any kind, did he?

ANDY: I didn't get into all that with him. He's
distraught. They're sending him to D C to testify. Can
you believe it? D C? Sven?

RICHARD: I better give him a call. Is he home?

ANDY: He was heading home. Just came in to...get
a few...pick up his son. *(Silence)* On the bright side,
they're saying smoking causes lung cancer. Whole big
article here. *(Silence)* The thing that drives me crazy is
the way they pick out some insignificant little guy ...
Don't misunderstand me, Sven's a fine man, but he's ...

RICHARD: I suppose they know that Communist
recruiters pick out the insignificant guys, guys like
algebra teachers.

ANDY: What... You're saying... What are you saying,
Dick? Sven Larsen's a Communist? Are you calling
him a Communist?

RICHARD: No, of course I'm not. I'm responding to
your comment that the little guys seem to take it in the
neck from these committees. Why would you accuse
me of calling Sven a Communist?

ANDY: It sounded like that's what you were saying.

RICHARD: Try not to jump to conclusions like that.
That's dangerous.

ANDY: Cops have to serve so many tickets a month.
Senators have to finger so many pinkos a month. It's a
goddamned quota.

RICHARD: And the best crooks obey the traffic laws.

ANDY: It's easy for you to be glib. It's easy for a war hero to sit back and poke fun. But if you think Sven's getting a kick out of—

RICHARD: What?

ANDY: What that poor guy and his family are going through—

RICHARD: What war hero?

ANDY: Okay, I'm going to tell you something. This is you and me here. I went to Michigan. You know that. I belonged to a study group there. Bunch of Jewish kids, went to synagogue together every Friday, studied the Talmud together.

RICHARD: Andy…

ANDY: We debated lots of philosophies. Schopenhauer. Kierkegaard. You know. Kicked ideas around.

RICHARD: Andy!

ANDY: Try to make a better world.

RICHARD: What war hero, Andy?

ANDY: Come on. Everybody knows.

RICHARD: Everybody knows what?

ANDY: It's nothing to be ashamed of.

RICHARD: What does everybody know?

ANDY: I know you're modest about it. I'm using it to make a point.

(Enter BAXTER.)

RICHARD: Modest about what?

ANDY: Your medal and all.

RICHARD: What else does everybody know, Drew?

BAXTER: We're all very proud of you, Dick.

RICHARD: I thought I made it clear that—

BAXTER: Now don't get—

ANDY: All I'm trying to say here is—

RICHARD: I thought our talk was confidential.

BAXTER: It was. It is.

ANDY: Drew, do you mind, I'm trying to make a point here if I may.

RICHARD: Andy knew all about this before you even talked to me.

ANDY: Dick, if you'll just hear me out—

RICHARD: Does he know about the other thing?

BAXTER: Of course not. Now, Dick, you're making too much—

ANDY: —all I'm saying here is you're the kind of guy doesn't worry about what the whole world's going to say. But I have to kind of worry because when I was younger I belonged to—

RICHARD: I really am disappointed, Drew.

ANDY: Dick, will you listen to me?

RICHARD: More than disappointed.

ANDY: I'm trying to explain to you—

BAXTER: I didn't publish a memo, for chrissake.

ANDY: Would you listen to me? Please? This is kind of worrying me—

BAXTER: I mentioned it to Andy here in passing.

RICHARD: In passing!

ANDY: Would you both just shut up for a minute?

RICHARD: You mean in the john? The hallway? The cafeteria line? Oh say Andy, Dick won the D S C. Can you believe it?

ANDY: Oh. Oh. Oh God. Oh. *(His nose starts to bleed)*

BAXTER: Oh, Andy, here, grab this napkin.

ANDY: Ice. Ice.

BAXTER: Dick, get Andy some ice ...

(RICHARD slides to the floor.)

BAXTER: What's the matter with you?

RICHARD: I can't...bl...bl...oh...

BAXTER: Lie down on the floor there, Dick. You're going to pass out.

ANDY: Maybe I better lie down.

BAXTER: I'm going to get you some ice, Andy. Easy does it. Tilt your head. Be right back. *(He hurries out.)*

(RICHARD and ANDY are stretched out on the floor.)

ANDY: I didn't mean to cause all this commotion.

RICHARD: Okay. Okay. Okay. Okay.

ANDY: I get nosebleeds when I'm agitated.

RICHARD: Uh huh. Uh huh. Uh huh.

ANDY: You all right over there?

RICHARD: Just...need...some...just...

ANDY: Put your head between your knees.

RICHARD: Doesn't work...for me...

(BAXTER is back with janitor's bucket filled with ice.)

BAXTER: Here you go, Andy. Much ice as you need. George was out in the hall mopping up some poor kid's vomit. He had his bucket handy. How are you, Dick?

RICHARD: Okay. Okay. Fine. Okay.

ANDY: Vomit did you say?

BAXTER: Ice slows down the bleeding.

RICHARD: No! No! Don't say...don't...say...

BAXTER: Don't say?

RICHARD: The word.

BAXTER: You mean "bleeding"?

ANDY: Don't, Drew. He doesn't like you to say that word.

RICHARD: I can't...stand... Please don't.

(Long, long silence)

ANDY: I'll be okay now.

BAXTER: What the hell brought that on?

ANDY: I get worked up.

BAXTER: That's a bloody mess. You have another shirt here?

ANDY: Drew, have a little consideration. Go make sure that puke's cleaned up. I'm fine now.

BAXTER: You want me to phone for an ambulance?

ANDY: Absolutely no necessity for that, Drew.

BAXTER: Dick? You need a cold cloth or anything?

RICHARD: Some of this ice. I'll just...

BAXTER: That's it. Put some of that ice on the back of your neck. Thank heavens Andy's stopped bleeding.

ANDY: We're fine, Drew. Really. Go. Leave. Now. Please.

RICHARD: And Drew? Don't make a thing of this. Okay? Don't go out there in the halls and make an announcement.

BAXTER: What do you think I am? *(He goes out.)*

RICHARD: There goes my contract for next year.

ANDY: I'm sorry I made you pass out.

RICHARD: My wife thinks I should see a shrink.

ANDY: Did you get that phobia in Italy?

RICHARD: I've always had this. When I was a kid, my sister fell out of a tree. I collapsed.

ANDY: Then how did you manage to...I mean, all those men, soldiers, who got...Italy and everything.

RICHARD: What are you afraid of?

ANDY: Snakes. My dad.

RICHARD: Your dad?

ANDY: He's a little Jewish man from Poland who has no country to go back to visit and wants absolutely the American Dream. Will not take no for an answer on the American Dream. Forgives Roosevelt for Poland and insists on the American Dream. "You should be President already." You should hear him. "Teaching English when you could be Secretary of State, do something important for the world." On and on.

RICHARD: They always want what they think is best for us.

ANDY: He's the world's gentlest man. But if he comes into a room where a light was left on...I'm not kidding, the veins on his neck stand out. He turns purple. "In Poland what they'd give for a little electricity and look how you waste. Look how you waste."

RICHARD: But you're not really scared of him.

ANDY: The committee. *(Silence)* I'm scared of the House committee.

RICHARD: You were trying to explain something to me before, about some group, some student group you joined.

ANDY: The committee's looking pretty hard at education. You've seen the papers. Now this Sven Larsen situation. They're bound to turn my name up.

RICHARD: You teach kids how to diagram sentences, how to use the semi-colon. How to scan iambic pentameter.

ANDY: Sven teaches square roots and how to prove theorems.

RICHARD: And apparently he knows some people.

ANDY: And I joined a study group in college.

RICHARD: To read the Torah.

(Silence)

ANDY: That, too.

RICHARD: That's what you said.

ANDY: That's what we did. Along with kicking around a few theories. You know, late at night, one idea leads to another, you get excited, stimulated, you say things. Try out radical notions on each other, see how they play out.

(Enter BARBARA.)

BARBARA: Drew said Dick passed out.

ANDY: Well, Drew's wrong.

BARBARA: Here's more Kleenex, Andy. Drew said you were bleeding like—

ANDY: Thank you. Everything is fine. Just absolutely okay.

BARBARA: I'm late for sixth period. *(She goes out.)*

(Silence)

RICHARD: Lung cancer. They sure about that?

(Lights out on RICHARD and ANDY as AGENT KIMBLE steps into central playing area and bright light on him)

AGENT KIMBLE: Please sit down. I'm Agent Kimble.

(RICHARD *steps into the downstage area where* AGENT KIMBLE *is waiting.*)

RICHARD: I received this. (*He holds out the summons.*)

AGENT KIMBLE: We appreciate this is inconvenient for you and your school.

RICHARD: I assume you've seen my curriculum.

AGENT KIMBLE: Can we get you a glass of water? Coffee?

(RICHARD *sits.*)

RICHARD: Is there any question about the curriculum?

AGENT KIMBLE: No. No question about your curriculum. None whatsoever.

RICHARD: I thought maybe you wanted to verify…

AGENT KIMBLE: Your curriculum is not in question at all.

RICHARD: Well… How can I help you?

AGENT KIMBLE: As you know, as most people know, a certain group hostile to our way of life is out to undermine us.

RICHARD: I'm not a Communist.

AGENT KIMBLE: No one's accusing you of that, sir.

RICHARD: I've never attended a meeting. Even by accident.

AGENT KIMBLE: You're not here to defend yourself against anything. Please don't have any compunction about any of that.

RICHARD: Is this in regard to Sven Larsen? He teaches at the same school I do. You've been interviewing him—

AGENT KIMBLE: Congress is concerned about the kinds of people in the education system in this country. You're aware, I'm sure, of the flap at the University of Michigan and Cal, professors who have taken a rather unpleasant stance about...their inalienable rights.

RICHARD: Yes. I've read about it.

AGENT KIMBLE: And so we're reviewing the records of a number of people at all levels of education.

RICHARD: I see.

AGENT KIMBLE: Your school is one of the institutions that have attracted our attention.

RICHARD: I don't understand.

AGENT KIMBLE: Mister Packard, you're a man entrusted with the minds of our young people, entrusted to teach them democracy. You served your country in the Italian campaign. You were awarded the Distinguished Service Cross. You've won a number of teaching awards. You are just the kind of man we want in our classrooms. And just the sort of citizen who could assist us in our endeavors.

RICHARD: What's wrong at my school?

AGENT KIMBLE: Have you observed anything in your colleagues' behavior that seemed inappropriate... suspicious?

RICHARD: If you mean Sven Larsen, there's absolutely no reason to suspect him of any kind of subversive—

AGENT KIMBLE: Actually, my question doesn't apply to Mister Larsen, whom I've not had the pleasure to meet. What I'm referring to is something slight in and of itself that may have set off an alarm bell for you. Something a little out of kilter, out of the ordinary. That caught your attention.

RICHARD: Is there somebody in particular? Why don't you speak to them directly?

AGENT KIMBLE: We're hoping there's nothing behind our information. This is where you can help us.

RICHARD: I'm not sure I understand what you want me to do.

AGENT KIMBLE: Report to us.

RICHARD: Report?

AGENT KIMBLE: On a weekly basis, say.

RICHARD: Of course if I saw someone planting a bomb in a locker I'd call you. But that's not going to happen.

AGENT KIMBLE: Maybe someone invites you to dinner with some…some people. Conversation is general, intelligent, and subtly turns onto certain philosophical or sociological grounds. Maybe someone drops a comment about…oh, something they've read recently, someone they had dinner with, a book club they joined. You know the sort of thing.

RICHARD: Anyone who gathers information about other people and reports that information to—

AGENT KIMBLE: It's concerned citizens who help us the most.

RICHARD: Forgive me. I don't mean to be combative, but what you're asking me to do is unconstitutional.

AGENT KIMBLE: The Bureau is a crime fighting organization. We're investigating conspirators determined to overthrow the United States government. A crime, would you say. We're asking you to perform a service for your country as part of that investigation. It's really quite straightforward. An extension, if you will, of the kind of dedicated service you gave during the war.

RICHARD: Why me in particular?

AGENT KIMBLE: An upstanding citizen with an impressive academic and military background. Trustworthy. Competent. Reliable. A civics teacher. Who better?

RICHARD: I don't think...I'm not sure I'd be very good at...

AGENT KIMBLE: You teach eighth graders about our system of government. What do you teach them?

RICHARD: I teach the curriculum for civics ratified by this state.

AGENT KIMBLE: Just a synopsis of that.

RICHARD: The three branches of government. Their duties. Some basic economics. The Constitution. Voting procedures. Immigration. Basically how the country works.

AGENT KIMBLE: Have you read the Communist Manifesto? *(He selects a paper from his file folder.)* You have proposed in faculty meetings, on more than one occasion, teaching the Isms.

RICHARD: What is that paper?

AGENT KIMBLE: I remind you, sir, you have nothing to defend here.

RICHARD: How do you know what gets tabled at faculty meetings?

AGENT KIMBLE: Can you list for me the Isms?

RICHARD: Fascism. Socialism. Totalitarianism. Capitalism. Communi—

AGENT KIMBLE: You propose teaching Communism in civics?

RICHARD: That's incorrect.

AGENT KIMBLE: Your name is Richard Alan Packard, isn't it. You are the Richard Packard who teaches civics in—

RICHARD: I should have a copy of that, shouldn't I?

(AGENT KIMBLE *hands* RICHARD *a copy of the page.*)

AGENT KIMBLE: So you don't want to teach Communism.

RICHARD: I would like to be allowed to teach about Communism.

AGENT KIMBLE: What in your view is the difference between teaching about it and teaching it?

RICHARD: Teaching it is showing students how to implement it in their daily lives. How to apply it. Teaching about it is laying out for the students what it is, what it entails, its features, its flaws.

AGENT KIMBLE: I'm not sure an eighth grader can make that distinction.

RICHARD: I teach about the judicial system. My students don't all go out and become lawyers.

AGENT KIMBLE: But some of them do.

RICHARD: Probably.

AGENT KIMBLE: Young minds. Easily seduced. Would you say? And say you were granted permission to teach about Communism. How is it you know enough about the subject to teach it? Have you yourself made a study of the Communist system? In any depth?

RICHARD: Agent Kimble, let me put it to you this way, if I may. We're in the middle of a polio epidemic in this country. Scientists are trying desperately to find a vaccine. To do that they have to understand what the polio virus is, how it strikes, why it's powerful, what makes it grow. Are we better off fearing polio or understanding it?

AGENT KIMBLE: Mister Packard, you may unwittingly know card carrying members of that organization I alluded to a moment ago. I stress unwitting.

RICHARD: I don't know anybody who's a Communist.

AGENT KIMBLE: But you wouldn't know they were Communists. They wouldn't tell you. Not right at first.

RICHARD: I don't know anyone.

AGENT KIMBLE: Grant me that you wouldn't necessarily know they were.

RICHARD: Granted.

AGENT KIMBLE: You and your wife attended a garden party a month ago. *(Silence)* Is that correct?

RICHARD: Yes.

AGENT KIMBLE: At the home of a well-respected philosophy professor. *(Silence)* Yes or no? *(Silence)* This man is a close personal friend. Professor Otto Benjamin Wittig. *(Pronounces the name with a W)* Am I pronouncing his name correctly?

RICHARD: I was majoring in philosophy for a while. He was my mentor.

AGENT KIMBLE: A mentor, if I'm correct, is someone who influences another person's thinking.

RICHARD: Professor Wittig's not a Communist. *(Pronounces name with a V)*

AGENT KIMBLE: How shall I put this? I could thank you for your time and send you home and ask the art teacher or the gym teacher or the shop teacher or someone else from your school to help us. But it seems to me that those people don't have as much at stake as you do. Would you say?

RICHARD: I don't understand you. At stake?

AGENT KIMBLE: There's really no reason for your name to come up in the Wittig investigation.

RICHARD: Professor Wittig is under investigation?

AGENT KIMBLE: If you need a day or two to think over what we've talked about…

RICHARD: He hasn't said anything about an investigation.

AGENT KIMBLE: This wouldn't be something to discuss with your wife. What with her recent…miscarriage. *(Silence)* So may your government count on you?

(Light out on AGENT KIMBLE *and bright on* RICHARD*)*

(Music by Prokoviev)

*(*ANDY *writes a new date on the chalk board.)*

(Lights on faculty room. RICHARD *stands alone in dismay.* BARBARA *comes in.)*

BARBARA: You heard. About Sven.

RICHARD: I…Sven?

BARBARA: They're letting him go. Effective immediately. Drew hired the sub to finish out the term.

RICHARD: Letting him go.

BARBARA: I know. It's just awful. They're letting him resign. It looks better on his record. But you and I know he won't get a teaching job anywhere now. Of course I suppose if they're satisfied with his testimony he could be reinstated. Could he, do you think? Teach again, I mean?

RICHARD: Marked man.

BARBARA: I'm going to drop over to his place. I don't know what I can do. I just want to let him know… Dick, I know this is an absolutely vile time to tell you. With everything you and Sandy have been through.

And now this horrible business about Sven. But I...I'm going to have a baby.

RICHARD: Oh.

BARBARA: I didn't want to say anything till I was sure.

RICHARD: That's just...wow.

BARBARA: I don't want anyone to know yet. I want to be sure I have a contract for next year. I'll just need some leave. But we are so happy. You can tell Sandy, of course. If you think it's a good time. I hope this doesn't make you feel...I don't want you two to be discouraged.

RICHARD: I won't say a word.

BARBARA: How is Sandy?

RICHARD: She's good. Much better. She wants us to try again.

BARBARA: I'm so glad. Say hi to her. *(She goes out.)*

(RICHARD stands alone in the room.)

(BAXTER comes in with a stack of files, sees RICHARD, and slips out again quietly.)

(RICHARD goes to faculty lounge phone, dials, makes sure he's alone, then:)

RICHARD: *(On phone)* It's Richard Packard. That's right. I don't know... The way we left things, I had to think, I had to give... Yes. Yes. I thought about everything we discussed and... Yes. I did hear a conversation at Professor Wittig's barbecue. This is very hard for me...I know you do, but it's... He's been a great... You do understand, this was no kind of conspiratorial... Nobody was suggesting anything or plotting or... It was just a philosophical discussion, but... They did use terms like "better society, better way of life, more for the masses" ...Academic chit-chat. Innocuous... phrases. Just... Yes. Yes. Yes. *(A moment. He hangs up.)*

(MAXINE *comes in.*)

MAXINE: Excuse me. Mister Packard? I know I'm not supposed to come in here. *(Silence)* Do you think I could interview you for the *Fandango*? About why you think it's important to study civics.

RICHARD: What?

MAXINE: Why you think civics is important to study.

RICHARD: Oh. Civics. Sure. I guess.

MAXINE: Great. When? *(Silence)* I really love you. I mean your class. I really love everything about your class.

RICHARD: Thanks.

MAXINE: I think I want to be a lawyer. Learning all about the court and stuff. So tomorrow? After school? For my interview?

RICHARD: Tomorrow's Saturday.

(MAXINE *waits. He is preoccupied and withdrawn. She waits a little longer. Then she exits.*)

END OF ACT ONE

ACT TWO

(Dates on chalk boards show it is a Wednesday in the week following ACT ONE.*)*

MAXINE: *(Sings)*
Oh Shenandoah, i long to hear you
Away, you rolling river
Oh shenandoah, I long to hear you

(Light on BARBARA *as she listens to* MAXINE*'s audition)*

MAXINE: Away, I'm bound away
Cross the wide Missouri.

BARBARA: I think we want to put that in B for you.

MAXINE: Did you want me to sing the rest?

BARBARA: That's fine for now. That's what I needed to hear. I'd like you to do the whole song for assembly.

MAXINE: Really? Can I?

BARBARA: I'll transpose the key. Make it more alto.

MAXINE: A solo?

BARBARA: We should schedule some rehearsal time.

MAXINE: I can come after school. Every day if you want.

BARBARA: Can you get some kind of costume together?

MAXINE: Mom can make me one.

BARBARA: Come see me next week and we'll set up rehearsals.

MAXINE: Oh, Mrs Penning, could I ask you… This is for the newspaper. I'm writing an essay about American education. You know how in your class you teach about composers. Why is that important?

BARBARA: I think it's important to understand something about the personality and the background of a composer so you can better appreciate the music he wrote.

MAXINE: But why?

BARBARA: Well, where does music come from?

MAXINE: I guess it comes from an idea you get for a tune. Then you sort of make up the tune and add on to it.

BARBARA: That's exactly right. Music comes from a creative spark within. Your composition comes out of who you are. And if the composer is deaf, as Beethoven was, then the music is informed by his affliction to some degree. And by his father's harshness to him. That's one example. We've been listening to Mussorgsky. I've been telling the class about events in his life which he tries to express in his music. I think you can appreciate the intensity of his music so much more when you know what a sad life he had.

MAXINE: But is it okay to listen to Russian music?

BARBARA: Any educated person should have exposure to all the masterpieces, regardless of nationality. Russians have a very unusual and special sensibility. You know, they come from an oppressed culture and out of that comes music with enormous vitality and passion.

MAXINE: But the Russians are our enemies.

BARBARA: Not the Russians you listen to in class.

MAXINE: But we shouldn't have to listen to Russian music, should we.

BARBARA: Maxine, are you particularly uncomfortable listening to Mussorgsky or Tchaikovsky?

MAXINE: Well…I like the music. Especially *Swan Lake*. But they are Communists.

BARBARA: These men lived long before the revolution.

MAXINE: I really like the course. But I'm just wondering if we should be listening to music by Russians.

BARBARA: The great thing about music is that it can transcend political and national and philosophical barriers. Think about this. *Nutcracker Suite*. The Opera Ballet puts it on every Christmas. That's a Russian story. But it's not about Communism. It's about a little girl who gets a wonderful gift for Christmas. Or *Peter and the Wolf,* where a little boy's courage saves his village.

MAXINE: Thanks. This was a big help.

(Lights out on MAXINE *and* BARBARA. *Up on* ANDY *and* BAXTER *in faculty lounge)*

ANDY: Drew, I've got to talk to you. I mean right now.

BAXTER: This is not a convenient…I have to meet with the P E people about the track meet.

ANDY: This won't wait.

BAXTER: All right. What's up?

ANDY: Dick Packard got one of those things, didn't he.

BAXTER: Things?

ANDY: Like Sven Larsen. From the F B I.

BAXTER: I don't think it amounted to anything. Don't tell me you got one.

ANDY: I signed the loyalty oath.

BAXTER: We all signed it. What's the problem?

ANDY: Drew, look, this Larsen situation.

BAXTER: It was no pleasure for me to see him go. He's one of my best teachers.

ANDY: Then why is he gone?

BAXTER: Sven felt it was better for him and for us if he went. You know this.

ANDY: Before he was sacked.

BAXTER: You said it. Not me.

ANDY: But you know it. You know what the school board would do. How long would the House committee let him stay in a classroom?

BAXTER: Let's presume innocence, shall we.

ANDY: Of course I presume innocence. Sven is innocent.

BAXTER: Meanwhile, I don't know the substance of Sven's conversation with the F B I. I don't know what they asked him. I don't know what he told them. I do know he came and asked me if he could leave.

ANDY: Sven isn't guilty of anything. The system just convicted him. The system's guilty.

BAXTER: You're pushing on an open door, Andy. It was Sven's decision. I didn't suggest he resign. I hated to lose him. He wanted to go. I don't know what the board would have decided. I don't make the rules. What can I say?

ANDY: What about you?

BAXTER: What about me?

ANDY: Are you called in?

BAXTER: Andy, this kind of paranoia is—

ANDY: Who turned Sven in?

BAXTER: Who turned… What?

ANDY: He's a quiet little Danish guy teaching math. There's no reason why he would have come to their attention in the first place. Unless somebody—

BAXTER: That is a damnable thing to imply.

ANDY: There's a fear permeating this whole school. Teachers are slinking around. The kids don't understand why Mr. Larsen suddenly isn't teaching algebra. You haven't addressed it in the assemblies. You haven't sent out any kind of leaflet for the students to take home. Even the *Fandango* hasn't addressed it. They should, but they're backing off. He's just not here anymore. He's gone. And his son's gone. Their classmate. Student body treasurer. Gone. And no explanation. As far as the student body knows, the whole Larsen family could be on their way to a gulag.

BAXTER: What are you accusing me of? Just say it.

ANDY: Who did you cave in to?

BAXTER: What kind of a thing is that to say to me?

ANDY: You're disappointed because they passed over your name for Superintendant of Schools. I don't blame you there. The fellow they got is useless. Worse than useless. He panders to… And to stay in the future running, you have to play a little ball. That's all I've got to say.

BAXTER: Play a little ball.

ANDY: If the shoe fits.

(BARBARA *enters.*)

BAXTER: Sell out one of my own teachers.

ANDY: Somebody did.

BAXTER: Is that what you think?

ANDY: Somebody had to.

BAXTER: Do you really think someone here would do a thing like that? And do it as a career move?

ANDY: I don't know what else to think.

BAXTER: Don't you dare get a bloody nose, you bastard. (*He exits.*)

(*Silence*)

BARBARA: You talk to Dick since his meeting?

ANDY: Just… Not really.

BARBARA: What was that about?

ANDY: Oh, it's about Drew and his… Sometimes how he won't…

BARBARA: I'm taking maternity leave fall term. I may just stay home for good.

ANDY: You mean, I mean, you're going to have a baby? Congratulations, Barbara. That is such great news.

BARBARA: I didn't hear all of that, Andy. And it's not my place, but you and I have been friends a long time. You were awfully rough on Drew.

ANDY: I'm sorry you had to hear that. It's a tough time for the Larsen family and rumors are racing all over the school, in case you haven't noticed. And somebody's responsible.

BARBARA: Do you really believe Drew would have the heart to turn Sven Larsen or anybody else on this faculty in to the authorities?

ANDY: I'd sure like to see Drew stop being avuncular long enough to take control of this school.

BARBARA: I know Drew can be exasperating. I know he gets flustered because he tries so hard to do his job right. But he's a gentleman, Andy. He's loyal to his staff. He hates confrontation about as much as I do, but he faces up to things when … You know what I'm saying. If Sven had chosen to stay here, Drew would have stood by him. Even against the school board. He would. I really believe he would. Letting Sven go must have just about killed him and I think you came down on him…

(*Lights on* ANDY, BARBARA, BAXTER, *and* RICHARD)

(*A new date on chalk board*)

(MAXINE *in western costume sings for the assembly*)

MAXINE:
Oh shenandoah, I love your daughter
Away, you rolling river
Oh Shenandoah, I love your daughter
Away, I'm bound away
Cross the wide Missouri.

BARBARA: (*Reads from school paper*) "Mrs Barbara Penning, who teaches Music and leads Glee Club and Choir, feels American students can learn a lot from listening to Russian music. She says the Russians have better musical training and a better ear for music than Americans. Mrs Penning says the more we learn about the lives of Russian composers the better American culture will be."

MAXINE:
Oh Shenandoah, I'm bound to leave you
Away, you rolling river
Oh shenandoah, I'll not deceive you
Away, I'm bound away
Cross the wide Missouri.

BARBARA: I didn't say that.

(*Light out on* MAXINE)

(*Light on faculty room. The four teachers converge.*)

BARBARA: She embellished. This is not what I said.

ANDY: It's a habit of hers.

BARBARA: She took the ideas we discussed and reinterpreted them. I didn't say these things. Not this way. Boy, if the wrong you-know-who gets hold of this—

BAXTER: Great assembly today, by the way.

BARBARA: Gee thanks.

BAXTER: Just excellent. The kids really enjoyed it. I heard them in the halls.

BARBARA: She makes me sound like I'm—

RICHARD: You could demand a retraction.

BAXTER: It's a junior high newspaper class. It's nothing.

RICHARD: It goes home. Parents see it.

ANDY: Beautiful, Dick. Make her cry, why not.

BARBARA: It's not Dick. It's… Why would Maxine…?

RICHARD: She's young. Idealistic. Hears what she wants to hear. I don't think she meant to misrepresent you.

BARBARA: She seems to enjoy the class.

RICHARD: That's why you've got to make the paper accountable. Put your precise ideas into the paper, rebut the article.

BARBARA: You know what! If they want me to teach Frank Sinatra and Frankie Laine and Frankenstein, I will. I'll do it. I'll do whatever they want. I just don't care.

BAXTER: You're blowing this out of—

BARBARA: No, he's right, Drew. He's right. People believe anything in print. My God, even our little school paper. If it's in the *Fandango* it might as well be in Sanskrit.

RICHARD: Demand a retraction right away. Don't let time pass on this.

BAXTER: They're working down the hall on the next issue. I can go with you, Barbara. If you really think all this is necessary.

BARBARA: Would you?

BAXTER: Yes. You bet. You bet I will.

(BAXTER *and* BARBARA *exit.*)

ANDY: Mean-spirited little brat.

RICHARD: You can't blame Maxine.

ANDY: She interviews someone. She gets it wrong. Of course I can blame her. She's a bright kid. She knows better. Evil little bitch.

RICHARD: She didn't misquote me.

ANDY: Maybe we all know how Maxine Hoyt feels about you.

RICHARD: Come on. She got carried away.

ANDY: Barbara's thinking about quitting teaching.

RICHARD: None of us can quit. Maxine made a mistake.

ANDY: Speaking of honest reporting in the newspapers, I saw the item about the philosophy department at the U. Isn't Ben Wittig a friend of yours?

RICHARD: Kind of.

ANDY: Did you know about this investigation?

RICHARD: I don't know him too well really. I took a class from him once.

ANDY: Say, how did your thing go? Your so-called sit-down.

RICHARD: It went.

ANDY: What did they want?

RICHARD: Curriculum.

ANDY: You filed and signed off on that twice. In triplicate.

RICHARD: They got hold of faculty meeting minutes.

ANDY: I guess the minutes are public record.

RICHARD: Nudged me about my ill-considered proposal to teach about the Isms.

ANDY: I had a hunch that would come back to bite you. But they cleared it up. You're finished with all that.

RICHARD: Oh. Yeah. They… just wanted … clarification. It was nothing really.

ANDY: But the F B I. Man.

RICHARD: He was… The agent I spoke to, he was actually very…

ANDY: Very?

RICHARD: Pleasant. Called me sir.

(BARBARA *returns.*)

BARBARA: Thank you, Dick. That felt good. I'm going to have a word with Maxine.

RICHARD: Good. Me, too. *(Silence)* She sings well, doesn't she.

(Light on AGENT KIMBLE *on phone.* RICHARD *picks up phone.)*

AGENT KIMBLE: Just so we're clear.

RICHARD: We are.

AGENT KIMBLE: You haven't phoned.

RICHARD: There wasn't any reason.

AGENT KIMBLE: We'd like to hear from you once a week. At least.

RICHARD: There's nothing to report.

AGENT KIMBLE: All the same, we'd like you to check in.

RICHARD: I understand.

AGENT KIMBLE: There may be nothing to report. I hope there isn't. I hope everything's fine at your school. But we can't be everywhere at once. So. We'll talk next week. Unless…

RICHARD: Yes. All right. This number?

AGENT KIMBLE: This number will reach me.

(*Light out on* AGENT KIMBLE)

(*Light on* RICHARD *in his classroom with* MAXINE)

MAXINE: But Mrs Penning said—

RICHARD: You didn't write what she said.

MAXINE: I wrote what she meant.

RICHARD: You remember what we've discussed in class about libel and slander? You remember what slander means?

MAXINE: In my notes.

RICHARD: Look it up.

MAXINE: Now?

(RICHARD *passes* MAXINE *a dictionary. She looks up a word.*)

MAXINE: Making a false statement that damages another person's reputation.

RICHARD: Libel.

(MAXINE *looks up the word.*)

MAXINE: Publishing a false statement that damages someone's reputation.

RICHARD: Which is what you did, Maxine. Or very nearly did. Unless you can back up your statements with solid evidence, about Mrs. Penning, about anybody, you can't write stuff like that.

MAXINE: Mister P, are you really mad at me?

RICHARD: The same rules apply here as they do in the outside world. You broke the law, Maxine.

MAXINE: But, see, she thinks...

RICHARD: Maxine, are you listening to me? You committed a felony offense. Whenever you repeat something someone said in your hearing, and you repeat it wrongly, or you embellish it, and by doing that you cause them harm, you're leaving yourself open to a lawsuit. Now in this case you've left yourself open to a very strong rebuttal. Which hurts your reputation and the *Fandango*'s reputation. And the school's reputation.

MAXINE: But everybody in school says Mister Larsen's a Communist and that's how come he got fired. Is that slander?

RICHARD: A good lawyer could make a strong case for slander if Mister Larsen decides to take this goddamned school to court! *(Silence)* I'm sorry, Maxine. That was out of order. Now, look, I don't think you meant to libel Mrs Penning. Neither does she.

MAXINE: But she said the Russians are better composers—

RICHARD: She says she did not say that. Maybe that's what you think you heard. You have to quote your source exactly. Not the way you want it to sound, but the way they said it.

MAXINE: But she thinks that the Russians—

RICHARD: You don't know what she thinks.

MAXINE: But she went to the Russian ballet when they came, you know, last month, and she kept saying how great they were.

RICHARD: What are you really trying to say in your article?

MAXINE: See… Maybe Mrs Penning's a Communist.

RICHARD: Maxine.

MAXINE: But maybe she is.

RICHARD: You would need a lot more than her enthusiasm for the ballet to make a case like that. A lot more.

MAXINE: Do you think it's true Mister Larsen's a Communist? Alex is really nice. But his father won't ever get to teach again.

RICHARD: Those are dangerous and irresponsible suppositions.

MAXINE: But you know what, that professor that's in all the newspapers and maybe he's a red and everything, he lives around the corner from me. He has all kinds of people come over. And nobody knows what they do at his house. They might be planning something really bad. Like maybe blowing up the governor's mansion or the university or something.

RICHARD: Maxine, let's stay on the subject here. I want you to apologize to Mrs Penning. And I want you to consider very carefully the difference between zealous reporting and honest reporting. Mrs Penning may be zealous about the Russian ballet. Maybe about Russian music in general. That's a matter of personal taste. Her ideas don't make her a Communist, and your ideas don't necessarily make you a good reporter. They are ideas. Just ideas. You can't indict someone for a thought. I hope we never will. Meanwhile, you can be prudent and considerate. And accurate in quoting someone.

MAXINE: I'll tell her I misunderstood.

RICHARD: Thank you.

MAXINE: Will this hurt my civics grade?

(MAXINE *exits.*)

(*Light on* BAXTER's *office*)

BAXTER: Calm down. Just...just...

(RICHARD *steps into* BAXTER's *space.*)

RICHARD: I don't know what kind of a shop you're running here, Drew.

BAXTER: The school board is publishing a position paper on this whole thing, which should allay any—

RICHARD: I just know every junior high kid is dying to read a position paper. They've decided Larsen's a red. I don't know if Barbara's rebuttal is going to have much impact on a student body that's taken to damning everyone who has an original thought or a personality or, God forbid, good taste.

BAXTER: What brought this on?

RICHARD: You mean my concern about the state of—

BAXTER: I had this same confrontation a few days ago with Andy Lawton. Maybe you two can get together and settle down.

RICHARD: I talked to Maxine Hoyt this morning about the Penning misquote and what she said made me realize how demoralized this whole damn student body has become.

BAXTER: What do you want me to do? What do you expect me to do?

RICHARD: Assemble the little brats. Put it to them straight.

BAXTER: I can't move on something like this without board approval.

RICHARD: Stick your head in the sand, please! Drew, you have got to step up. You've got to take command here.

BAXTER: This is really none of your business, but you might like to know that I was called on the carpet for the emergency faculty meeting I called when Sven was first summoned. I was informed in no uncertain terms that what I did exceeded my authority. Does that appease your concerns about my competence?

RICHARD: I'm sorry. Of course I didn't know. It's just that the school's... So often you back down.

(Light on BARBARA *in her classroom)*

BARBARA: Dick, is there anybody out in the hall?

BAXTER: Dick, I'm going to ask you to leave my office.

RICHARD: Look at the mess!

BAXTER: Just go, if you would.

BARBARA: I've got to talk to somebody about this. I don't know what to do.

RICHARD: Drew, I'm... The kids, the things they're saying about Sven and...and Benjamin Wittig.

BAXTER: Richard, I would appreciate it if you have anymore complaints about the way I do my job that you please take them directly to the school board.

(RICHARD *crosses into* BARBARA's *classroom.)*

BARBARA: I don't know what to do about this. I went over to see the Larsens. You know, show of support.

RICHARD: I was over there a couple of nights ago.

BARBARA: Did Sven say anything to you about what the F B I asked him?

RICHARD: I didn't like to press him too hard on all that.

BARBARA: Well, he didn't say much to me, either. But in the kitchen Anna told me something. I don't know whether to do anything about this or not. I don't know who else to talk to but you.

RICHARD: Should you tell me?

BARBARA: Anna told me for a reason. I think she's hoping I'll do something.

RICHARD: What did she say?

BARBARA: You can't say a word about this. Unless you think we should tell someone. Drew or somebody. Together maybe.

RICHARD: You've got my word.

BARBARA: They asked him if there was anyone here in school that Sven could...well, turn in.

RICHARD: I thought Sven's situation was because of people he knew in Europe.

BARBARA: Anna didn't mention that. She did say, and this is terrifying if she's accurate; she said they may have their eye on somebody in the school and that Sven could help his own case if he were to... You know.

RICHARD: Did she say who?

BARBARA: Anna doesn't know. Do you think someone here is really being surveilled?

RICHARD: No. No, that couldn't be.

BARBARA: I think we should tell Drew.

RICHARD: No.

BARBARA: But wouldn't it help Sven?

RICHARD: You heard this from his wife. She's under a lot of strain. She may have misunderstood.

BARBARA: Of course she didn't misunder—

RICHARD: He may not have told her everything. There's a wider context that we don't know anything about. I think… No. Let's just drop it.

BARBARA: But I know Anna's hoping I can do something, help Sven—

RICHARD: Anna's desperate. Of course she is. But it's Sven's place to take this up with Drew. Or the person involved. If he knows who that person is.

BARBARA: But who can it be? And why?

RICHARD: Barbara, don't start that. That kind of thinking is… We're a faculty. We can't start suspecting each other. Sven's kept his mouth shut. Let's honor that. That's the least we can do for him.

BARBARA: You're sure.

(*Light on* AGENT KIMBLE)

RICHARD: Really, Barbara. Don't touch this. Walk away.

BARBARA: Okay.

AGENT KIMBLE: Have you read the Communist Manifesto?

RICHARD: Agreed?

BARBARA: Thanks.

AGENT KIMBLE: It's a simple question.

RICHARD: For all we know, for all Sven knows, for all anyone knows, there's nobody. It's their way. They try to enlist you.

BARBARA: Did they try to enlist you?

RICHARD: There's nobody, Barbara. Nobody.

AGENT KIMBLE: Have you read it?

(RICHARD *enters the F B I space as lights go out on* BARBARA.)

RICHARD: Have you read the First Amendment?

AGENT KIMBLE: Mister Packard, what I have to say is rather delicate. I don't quite know how to put it without seeming... We... The Bureau don't feel that you're taking this seriously enough.

RICHARD: Taking what seriously.

AGENT KIMBLE: Your commitment to this project.

RICHARD: I turned in a man who treated me like a son. I take that very seriously.

AGENT KIMBLE: What we want from you are regular reports—

RICHARD: I haven't seen or heard anything other than a distraught bunch of kids making wild assumptions—

AGENT KIMBLE: —on any and all—

RICHARD: Nothing worth reporting! I can't make up stuff!

AGENT KIMBLE: Let me finish, please, sir. We want notes from you on faculty meetings, lunch room conversations, etc.

RICHARD: Do you really want a rehash of next year's budget?

AGENT KIMBLE: Trivial or no.

RICHARD: The approval of the next term play, every single student assembly performance? The track team results, the football scores? Do you really want to wade through pages of that kind of thing? Listen, Agent Kimble, if I uncover a conspiracy, I will be red hot on the phone to you. Trust me for that.

AGENT KIMBLE: You have a passion for teaching.

RICHARD: I don't know why you keep browbeating me.

AGENT KIMBLE: So there sit thirty kids, age thirteen, fourteen, learning all about how our government works, from a guy they think is pretty special. And maybe one student gets all inspired and drops into the library and starts poking around.

RICHARD: Library?

AGENT KIMBLE: Reads something that confuses…

RICHARD: You want kids to stop going to the library?

(AGENT KIMBLE *produces a paperback book and hands it to* RICHARD.)

RICHARD: *Official Rules of Football?*

AGENT KIMBLE: Take a look.

(RICHARD *opens book, leafs through several pages.*)

RICHARD: My God.

AGENT KIMBLE: Supposing that was sitting on the library shelf in Litchfield, Minnesota or Cheyenne, Wyoming, or in New York City, or in your public library right here.

RICHARD: What is this?

AGENT KIMBLE: What it looks like. Instructions on making bombs. Planting bombs. Starting fires. How to cripple industrial plants. There's a whole chapter on how to short circuit New York City's electrical supply.

RICHARD: Where did this come from?

AGENT KIMBLE: We confiscated crates of these books the night they were smuggled into the United States.

RICHARD: This is the virus I was talking about the first time we met. This you can fight. What you want from me isn't… This is real.

AGENT KIMBLE: You know how we were able to intercept this shipment? A tip-off. From a citizen. These people are slick, Mister Packard. Make no mistake.

They are brilliant. Masters. I only hope we have the resources to beat them. People get really attracted to—

RICHARD: You're afraid.

AGENT KIMBLE: Yes, sir. I am afraid.

RICHARD: You're scared their system is, what, superior, more powerful than ours?

AGENT KIMBLE: I know it's not.

RICHARD: I don't know who taught you civics, but you don't know. You don't know what Communism is, so it terrifies… Oh man. Oh my God. I've been so scared for myself all these weeks.

(AGENT KIMBLE *takes the book and slams it on the table.*)

AGENT KIMBLE: I know what Communism is! That is Communism!

RICHARD: The most brilliantly designed system of government on earth. You serve it but you don't trust it.

AGENT KIMBLE: No, sir. It's you who don't trust it. It's you who keep trying to improve it and redesign it or destroy it altogether. It's the people who take the trouble to cooperate with us, who furnish us with information, names, license plate numbers, bank records…

RICHARD: What?

AGENT KIMBLE: Those people who give enough of a damn about our system who really make it work.

RICHARD: Agent Kimble, you must know that if there were something, really something, a book like this at our school, of course I'd report it. To you. To my principal. To the school board. To the governor. If there really were something wrong, if I'd observed something, overheard something like this… (*He indicates the book.*) Your tipster, your citizen, did the country a great service. But he knew. See? He knew, for whatever reason, how I don't know, he knew those crates were coming into the country and that they contained subversive literature. Don't you see? That's the difference. I don't know about any wrongdoing. I'm just spying.

AGENT KIMBLE: Please, Mister Packard. Help me do my job. There's someone on your faculty. I know you know who it is. Knowing your background, I can't think of a reason why you'd be shielding this person.

RICHARD: I don't know what you're talking about.

AGENT KIMBLE: Give me his name.

RICHARD: I don't know…

AGENT KIMBLE: One name. One name and it's over. We won't trouble you again.

RICHARD: I don't know any name. What name? What name do you want?

AGENT KIMBLE: Give me Wladyslaw. (*Pronounces it WAHD-is-law*)

RICHARD: Even if I knew who that is.

AGENT KIMBLE: You know who it is. (*Silence*) Andrew Lawton is what he calls himself.

RICHARD: Oh Jesus. No. No. I will not. You are so wrong…I won't give him to you.

AGENT KIMBLE: Has this man ever said anything to you about his…his personal…shall we call them "preferences"?

RICHARD: No. Never. He never has.

AGENT KIMBLE: Do this for yourself, for your wife, if you won't for your country.

RICHARD: Andy Lawton's a good teacher. A fine teacher.

AGENT KIMBLE: His sexual practices, however...

RICHARD: His sexual...?

AGENT KIMBLE: It's the perverts, sir. The most vulnerable in our society that they go after. It's the perverts they convert first.

RICHARD: I don't know anything about any of this.

AGENT KIMBLE: I see that you mean well, Mister Packard. I know he's a friend.

RICHARD: Andy Lawton's not a Communist. That's all I know. You want to swear me in and depose me, that's what I can say under oath because that is God's truth.

AGENT KIMBLE: He's a colleague, a friend. You don't want to betray him. But this man is a teacher. This man is vulnerable to our enemies and to himself, and he is standing in a classroom teaching our children.

RICHARD: I have no name to give you.

AGENT KIMBLE: Would it make a difference to your decision if I told you I...we...know about your decoration? *(Silence)* I mean all about it. *(Silence)* You're a man who is in a position to help us, and for some misguided reason, some principled reason, I'm sure, you won't. And it would truly disappoint me to have to expose the facts about your citation for valor.

RICHARD: Yes! Yes, I have read the *Communist Manifesto*. I have also read *Das Kapital*. I live in a country where I can read anything I want.

AGENT KIMBLE: Don't do this, Mister Packard.

RICHARD: You do what you have to do.

AGENT KIMBLE: Don't do this.

RICHARD: Let your record show that I invoke my First and Fifth Amendment rights.

AGENT KIMBLE: The House committee has your brief. This discussion will be added to it. I don't know what will happen now. That part's out of my hands. I just don't know what to say to you. You don't seem to see what's happening; you don't seem to recognize the threat.

(RICHARD *reaches out his hand*).

RICHARD: Thank you for everything, Agent Kimble. I honestly mean this. I see how deeply committed you are to what you're doing.

(AGENT KIMBLE *and* RICHARD *shake hands.*)

RICHARD: You stand for everything I oppose, but, man, that's your perfect right in the land of the free and the home of the brave.

(*Enter* BAXTER *in his office area.*)

AGENT KIMBLE: I'm so sorry, Mister Packard. I'm so sorry.

RICHARD: You've given me every break, you've cut me as much slack as you dared. You've been patient with me and civil to me. And for that I thank you. But you've got to understand, if I keep on doing... My students wouldn't want me back in the classroom.

BAXTER: Richard. My office.

AGENT KIMBLE: If I could do anything to... but...

RICHARD: I just can't go along.

(*Light out on* AGENT KIMBLE *as* RICHARD *turns into* BAXTER'*s office*)

BAXTER: Richard... What's happened?

RICHARD: About what?

BAXTER: The school board called me.

RICHARD: Wow. That's quick.

BAXTER: Sit down.

RICHARD: I don't think I'll be here that long.

BAXTER: The FBI has sent a...

RICHARD: Yeah. I know.

BAXTER: I don't understand.

RICHARD: Do you want me to resign or do you want to do the honors?

BAXTER: They want me to suspend...

RICHARD: Effective when?

BAXTER: Until certain things are cleared up.

RICHARD: You want me to finish the semester?

BAXTER: Yes. Stay through finals. Turn in your grades.

RICHARD: Thank you for telling me yourself, Drew. Better than I deserve from you.

BAXTER: Is this about the medal?

RICHARD: It's all about the medal.

(RICHARD *goes to his classroom and begins packing books and files into a carton.*)

(*Light out on* BAXTER)

(BARBARA *writes a new date on the board, early June, two weeks later.*)

(*After a moment,* ANDY *enters* RICHARD's *classroom.*)

ANDY: You can sue.

RICHARD: She didn't know what it would mean. She didn't realize what she was doing.

ANDY: So you lose your job.

RICHARD: So I lose my job.

ANDY: And Professor Wittig and his colleagues get suspended without pay.

RICHARD: Yes.

ANDY: And she gets to go to ninth grade.

RICHARD: That's it.

ANDY: Look, can I ask you something out of line?
Did they ask you to cooperate with them in any way?
Could you have avoided this?

RICHARD: Andy, if you were out in the parking lot
burrowing under the hood of my car, taking my
battery out, I'd have a moral duty to blow the whistle
on you. I'd have to turn you in.

(Silence)

ANDY: We weren't a movement, for God's sake. We
weren't official. Maybe it was the country clubs we
couldn't join. The changing our names to sound like
we belonged. My father's accent. My mother's clothes.
A better society. A better world. A kinder world. That's
what we talked about. It wasn't Communism. Idealism,
maybe. Is that an Ism you can teach? That's all it was.
The Bureau wants you to rat me out for that?

RICHARD: Or I could go buy a new battery.

ANDY: Or is it something else? *(Silence)* I see.

RICHARD: Andy, I want you to know how I got my
medal.

ANDY: They want me for that.

RICHARD: You asked me how I stood it in Italy when
I can't even be in the room with you when your nose
starts to bl...

ANDY: Give me up, Dick. Save yourself.

RICHARD: Let me say that I sat in the mud on that beach
and let better men, my own men, enlisted guys, my
sergeant, my corporal, let them pull it off, let them stick
their necks out. They took the objective. They took the

beating. I took the credit. Professor Wittig. You asked me if I knew about his investigation. That man helped me through some really rough times right after the war. That man was a father to me. And I told you I hardly knew him. Save myself? What's to save?

ANDY: Does he know?

RICHARD: That I sold him out? That I denied his friendship?

ANDY: Are you going to tell him?

RICHARD: Man, if I can, I will have earned that medal.

ANDY: Does he have to know?

RICHARD: How do you pronounce your name?

ANDY: vlah DEES lahf. AHN jay vlah DEES lahf.

RICHARD: Good luck next year. Andy Lawton.

ANDY: What about Maxine?

RICHARD: Maxine gets an A.

ANDY: That's un-American.

RICHARD: Watch those nosebleeds.

(RICHARD *has said the taboo word.* ANDY *and* RICHARD *both react*)

(ANDY *exits.*)

(MAXINE *steps into* RICHARD's *classroom. He is at the chalk board and doesn't turn around*)

RICHARD: Your paper's on the desk, Maxine.

(MAXINE *picks up the folder.*)

RICHARD: Do you know why I'm leaving?

MAXINE: I didn't know you were leaving.

RICHARD: The man who lives around the corner from you.

MAXINE: What man?

RICHARD: He's a very dear friend of mine.

MAXINE: The professor? You know him?

RICHARD: The license plates.

MAXINE: What license plates?

RICHARD: The ones you turned in. It's in your report.

MAXINE: I don't understand.

RICHARD: I know you don't. I know.

MAXINE: The policeman told us to write down the license numbers.

RICHARD: A police officer told you to do that?

MAXINE: You mean you're not going to teach here anymore?

(This is the first time RICHARD *turns around and looks at* MAXINE.)

RICHARD: What did he tell you you were doing?

MAXINE: Getting license numbers of people who were Communists.

RICHARD: My car was parked there.

MAXINE: Your car?

RICHARD: What did the police officer tell you they'd done? Doctor Wittig's guests. What crimes were they charged with?

MAXINE: He said Doctor Wittig was teaching Communism at the university.

RICHARD: Does he take a course from Doctor Wittig?

MAXINE: We did what he told us.

RICHARD: Just obeying orders.

MAXINE: They won't fire you. Not 'cause of that.

RICHARD: Listen, Maxine.

MAXINE: You didn't do anything wrong.

RICHARD: I want you to listen to me very closely.

MAXINE: We didn't know you were there.

RICHARD: I don't want you to blame yourself. I want you to try very hard…

MAXINE: I'll tell Mister Baxter what happened.

RICHARD: Listen to me, Maxine.

MAXINE: I can explain that we were just… Who should I tell?

RICHARD: Turn this thing around or it will eat at you forever.

MAXINE: I can write something in the *Fandango*. I can make them listen to me.

RICHARD: That's what I want you to do. With your vote. With your taxes. From now on, forevermore, make them listen to you. The government is yours, Maxine. It works for you. You don't work for it.

MAXINE: They won't fire you, Mister P. They can't fire you.

RICHARD: We've got a good system, Maxine. Make it work.

MAXINE: We were pretending…

RICHARD: Good luck in ninth grade.

MAXINE: We were pretending to be spies. *(She hesitates, drops her report in the waste basket, and exits.)*

(RICHARD writes on the chalk board the words: "If you don't stand up for something, you will fall for anything". (He picks up his carton and his jacket and exits.)

(Brief light on chalk board. Blackout)

END OF PLAY

www.ingramcontent.com/pod-product-compliance
Lightning Source LLC
Chambersburg PA
CBHW060556100426
42742CB00013B/2583